SCHOLASTIC

SUPER SUDOKU MATH

MULTIPLICATION & DIVISION FACTS

Eric Charlesworth

I dedicate this book to all my students. Your positive attitudes toward learning fill every class with exciting possibilities! –E. C.

Editor: Sarah Longhi
Cover designer: Jason Robinson
Interior designer: Kelli Thompson
Illustrator: Teresa Anderko

ISBN-13: 978-0-545-15045-3
ISBN-10: 0-545-15045-0

1 2 3 4 5 6 7 8 9 10   40   16 15 14 13 12 11 10

New York • Toronto • London • Auckland • Sydney
Mexico City • New Delhi • Hong Kong • Buenos Aires

Teaching *Resources*

Contents

Introduction

Welcome to a new type of math practice that will engage students of all levels while reinforcing critical skills for math success!

As a middle-school math teacher, I see firsthand how students who are unable to do basic operations quickly encounter serious challenges with more sophisticated math work. Students who have trouble with automaticity tend to get overwhelmed by the more demanding (and more interesting) concepts and problem solving they face in middle school. It is no wonder that so many of these students harbor negative attitudes toward math as they realize the importance of the skills they lack. I work with students to help them overcome these difficulties in my classroom, using puzzles and games like the ones in this book. I'm eager to share these tools so that we can better support struggling students before they arrive in middle school.

In its Standards & Focal Points document (2006), the National Council of Teachers of Mathematics advises that students gain computational fluency with multiplication and division in the elementary grades. This book is designed to provide the type of engaging work with repeated practice that helps students achieve mastery. You can replace most rote facts-practice worksheets with the 41 leveled Sudoku puzzle challenges in this collection. Here are some key advantages to using these puzzles:

1 They promote algebraic reasoning and build understanding of the inverse relationship between multiplication and division.

___ **x 9 = 54** is just one step away from **9x = 54**.

2 They provide multiple pathways to finding the right answer, which supports flexible thinking.

3 They encourage students to use trial-and-error and deductive reasoning to find the solution, thus building problem-solving skills while supporting automaticity with basic facts.

4 The puzzles are self-checking. Students feel empowered when they do them. If everything comes out right, they feel good. If they make an error, they will quickly find that the puzzle isn't working, which will help them catch the mistake and try to correct it themselves.

5 Students who have struggled with rote, repetitive sheets are tired of them. The more advanced students, who breeze through those sheets, are also sick of them. With this book, all students get a new window into facts practice.

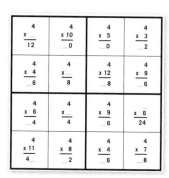

Regular-sized puzzle

Super-sized puzzle

How to Use This Book

These puzzles can be used flexibly. You may want to hand out copies of the puzzles for a warm-up activity (or "do now") to start class. However, they can also be given to students who finish their class work early or occasionally as homework.

Best of all, it is easy to differentiate with this book.

The super-sized Sudoku puzzles (6-by-6 grids) are more complex than the regular-sized puzzles (4-by-4 grids) and can be given to students who are ready for the challenge. Here are some additional ways to meet the needs of the diverse learners in your classroom.

Suggested challenge activities:

- Have students solve the Word Problems that appear at the bottom of some of the puzzle pages.
- Time students to see how quickly they can complete the puzzles—and beat their own best times. (Make sure this is done in a non-competitive, non-public way.)
- Have students create their own Sudoku puzzle to give to their classmates. Once they are familiar with the format, some students will love doing this.

Suggested support for struggling students:

- Have them practice with easy-level standard Sudoku puzzles first to build their confidence with the format.
- Model or solve puzzles as a class on the overhead or the interactive whiteboard.
- Allow students to refer to the Multiplication Table on page 5. (You may enlarge the table as needed.)
- Use the tips included at the bottom of some of the Sudoku puzzle pages.

Another way to differentiate is to allow some students practice with the puzzles in this book while students who are more secure with these facts try puzzles from the companion books *Super Sudoku Math: Fractions & Decimals* and *Super Sudoku Math: Addition & Subtraction Facts*.

NCTM Standard Connection

The student will

- understand various meanings of multiplication and division
- understand the effects of multiplying and dividing whole numbers
- identify and use relationships between operations, such as division as the inverse of multiplication, to solve problems

Multiplication Table

×	0	1	2	3	4	5	6	7	8	9	10	11	12
0	0	0	0	0	0	0	0	0	0	0	0	0	0
1	0	1	2	3	4	5	6	7	8	9	10	11	12
2	0	2	4	6	8	10	12	14	16	18	20	22	24
3	0	3	6	9	12	15	18	21	24	27	30	33	36
4	0	4	8	12	16	20	24	28	32	36	40	44	48
5	0	5	10	15	20	25	30	35	40	45	50	55	60
6	0	6	12	18	24	30	36	42	48	54	60	66	72
7	0	7	14	21	28	35	42	49	56	63	70	77	84
8	0	8	16	24	32	40	48	56	64	72	80	88	96
9	0	9	18	27	36	45	54	63	72	81	90	99	108
10	0	10	20	30	40	50	60	70	80	90	100	110	120
11	0	11	22	33	44	55	66	77	88	99	110	121	132
12	0	12	24	36	48	60	72	84	96	108	120	132	144

How to use this table

Multiplication:

Example: To find **8 × 3:**

1. Go down to the **"8"** row.

2. Follow the **"8"** row across to meet the **"3"** column.

3. Find your answer: **24**!

Division:

Example: To find **12 ÷ 4:**

1. Go across to the **"4"** column.

2. Go down to find the dividend **12**.

3. Go back across the row to find your answer: **3**!

Super SUDOKU RULES

Regular-sized Puzzles

Rule 1

1	2	3	4
3	4	1	2
2	1	4	3
4	3	2	1

▶ Fill in the **row** so that it contains numbers 1 through 4.

Rule 2

1	2	3	4
3	4	1	2
2	1	4	3
4	3	2	1

▶ Fill in the **column** so that it contains numbers 1 through 4.

Rule 3

1	2	3	4
3	4	1	2
2	1	4	3
4	3	2	1

▶ Fill in the 2-by-2 **box** so that it contains the numbers 1 through 4.

Super-sized Puzzles

Rule 1

1	2	3	4	5	6
3	4	1	2	6	5
2	1	5	3	4	6
4	5	6	1	2	3
6	2	4	5	1	3
2	5	1	4	3	6

▶ Fill in the **row** so that it contains numbers 1 through 6.

Rule 2

1	2	3	4	5	6
2	4	1	2	6	5
3	1	5	3	4	6
4	5	6	1	2	3
5	2	4	5	1	3
6	5	1	4	3	6

▶ Fill in the **column** so that it contains numbers 1 through 6.

Rule 3

1	2	3	4	5	6
4	5	6	2	6	5
2	1	5	3	4	6
4	5	6	1	2	3
6	2	4	5	1	3
2	5	1	4	3	6

▶ Fill in the 3-by-2 **box** so that it contains the numbers 1 through 6.

TIP!

For many of the regular-sized puzzles in this book, you will fill in the spaces with the numbers 5, 6, 7 and 8 instead of 1, 2, 3 and 4. All other rules remain the same.

Super Sudoku Math: Addition & Subtraction Facts • © 2010 by Eric Charlesworth • Scholastic Teaching Resources

Name _____ Date _____

Multiplying by 1

Directions

- Every row, column, and 2-by-2 box ⊞ should contain each of these digits:

  1 2 3 4

- Fill in each blank with the correct number to complete the fact.

$\begin{array}{r} 1 \\ \times\ 3 \\ \hline \end{array}$	$\begin{array}{r} 1 \\ \times\ \underline{\ \ }2 \\ \hline 12 \end{array}$	$\begin{array}{r} 1 \\ \times\ \underline{\ \ } \\ \hline 4 \end{array}$	$\begin{array}{r} 1 \\ \times\ 1\underline{\ \ } \\ \hline 12 \end{array}$
$\begin{array}{r} 1 \\ \times\ \underline{\ \ } \\ \hline 2 \end{array}$	$\begin{array}{r} 1 \\ \times\ 4 \\ \hline \end{array}$	$\begin{array}{r} \underline{\ \ } \\ \times\ 8 \\ \hline 8 \end{array}$	$\begin{array}{r} 1 \\ \times\ \underline{\ \ } \\ \hline 3 \end{array}$
$\begin{array}{r} 1 \\ \times\ \underline{\ \ } \\ \hline 4 \end{array}$	$\begin{array}{r} 1 \\ \times\ 2 \\ \hline \end{array}$	$\begin{array}{r} 1 \\ \times\ \underline{\ \ } \\ \hline 3 \end{array}$	$\begin{array}{r} \underline{\ \ } \\ \times\ 10 \\ \hline 10 \end{array}$
$\begin{array}{r} 1 \\ \times\ \underline{\ \ } \\ \hline 1 \end{array}$	$\begin{array}{r} 1 \\ \times\ 3 \\ \hline \end{array}$	$\begin{array}{r} 1 \\ \times\ 12 \\ \hline 1\underline{\ \ } \end{array}$	$\begin{array}{r} 1 \\ \times\ 4 \\ \hline \end{array}$

Tip!

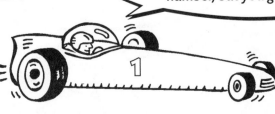

Multiplying by 1 does not change your original number. So 17 bazookazillion times 1 is still 17 bazookazillion. No, it's not a real number, but you get my point!

Name _____ Date _____

Multiplying by **2**

Directions

● Every row, column, and 2-by-2 box ⊞ should contain each of these digits:

5   **6**   **7**   **8**

● Fill in each blank with the correct number to complete the fact.

2 x __ —— 10	2 x __ —— 12	2 x 9 —— 1_	2 x __ —— 14
2 x __ —— 14	2 x __ —— 16	2 x 8 —— 1_	2 x __ —— 10
2 x 4 ——	2 x __ —— 10	2 x __ —— 14	2 x __ —— 12
2 x 3 ——	2 x __ —— 14	2 x __ —— 10	2 x 9 —— 1_

Tip!

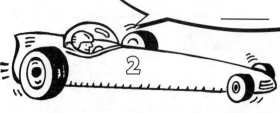

Multiplying by 2 is also called doubling. If I had six dollars and I doubled my money, how much money do I have now?

_____

Super Sudoku Math: Multiplication & Division Facts • © 2010 by Eric Charlesworth • Scholastic Teaching Resources

Super SUDOKU

Name _____ Date _____

Multiplying by 3

Directions

● Every row, column, and 2-by-2 box ⊞ should contain each of these digits:

1 2 3 4

● Fill in each blank with the correct number to complete the fact.

3 x 11 ___ __ 3	3 x 7 ___ 2 __	3 x ___ ___ 12	3 x 1__ ___ 36
3 x 9 ___ __ 7	3 x 8 ___ 2 __	3 x 5 ___ __ 5	3 x ___ ___ 9
3 x 8 ___ 2 __	3 x ___ ___ 6	__ x 6 ___ 18	3 x ___ ___ 3
3 x 5 ___ __ 5	__ x 12 ___ 36	3 x 9 ___ __ 7	3 x ___ ___ 12

Tip!

The answer to a multiplication problem is called a product. What's the product of 3 and 9?

_____

Super SUDOKU

Name _____ Date _____

Multiplying by 4

Directions

● Every row, column, and 2-by-2 box ⊞ should contain each of these digits:

1   2   3   4

● Fill in each blank with the correct number to complete the fact.

4 x __ ――― 12	4 x 10 ――― _0	4 x 5 ――― _0	4 x 3 ――― _2
4 x 4 ――― _6	4 x __ ――― 8	4 x 12 ――― _8	4 x 9 ――― _6
4 x 6 ――― _4	4 x __ ――― 4	4 x 9 ――― _6	__ x 6 ――― 24
4 x 11 ――― 4_	4 x 8 ――― _2	4 x 4 ――― _6	4 x 7 ――― _8

Word Problem

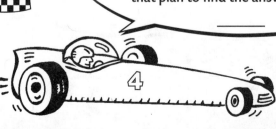

The trick to multiplying by 4? Simply double the number and then double it again. Use that plan to find the answer to 20 x 4.

_____

Super Sudoku Math: Multiplication & Division Facts • © 2010 by Eric Charlesworth • Scholastic Teaching Resources

Name _____ Date _____

Multiplying by **1, 2, 3,** and **4**

Directions

● Every row, column, and 3-by-2 box ⊞ should contain each of these digits:

1   **2**   **3**   **4**   **5**   **6**

● Fill in each blank with the correct number to complete the fact.

4 x __ 8	4 x __ 16	2 x __ 6	4 x 4 __6	2 x __ 10	3 x 2 __
3 x 5 1__	3 x 4 __2	3 x __ 18	3 x 11 3__	3 x 8 __4	4 x 10 __0
3 x 12 __6	4 x 7 __8	2 x 7 __4	3 x 8 2__	4 x __ 24	1 x __ 5
4 x 12 8	2 x 8 1__	3 x __ 15	4 x 5 __0	4 x 8 __2	1 x 1 __
4 x 4 1__	3 x __ 9	2 x __ 8	4 x __ 20	3 x 5 __5	3 x __ 6
3 x 7 2__	2 x __ 10	2 x 12 __4	4 x 9 3__	1 x __ 4	4 x 9 __6

Super SUDOKU

Name _____ Date _____

Multiplying by **5**

Directions

● Every row, column, and 2-by-2 box ⊞ should contain each of these digits:

1 **2** **3** **4**

● Fill in each blank with the correct number to complete the fact.

5 x 1 _ ――― 55	5 x _ ――― 20	5 x _ ――― 15	5 x 1 _ ――― 60
5 x 4 ――― _ 0	5 x 7 ――― _ 5	5 x 8 ――― _ 0	5 x _ ――― 5
5 x 8 ――― _ 0	5 x 3 ――― _ 5	5 x 5 ――― _ 5	5 x 6 ――― _ 0
5 x 6 ――― _ 0	5 x _ ――― 10	5 x _ 0 ――― 50	5 x 9 ――― _ 5

Tip!

Every time you multiply by 5 the product will end with either a 0 or a 5. That's because 5 goes into 10 twice evenly.

Super Sudoku Math: Multiplication & Division Facts • © 2010 by Eric Charlesworth • Scholastic Teaching Resources

Name _____   Date _____

Multiplying by **6**

Directions

- Every row, column, and 2-by-2 box ⊞ should contain each of these digits:

  1   **2**   **3**   **4**

- Fill in each blank with the correct number to complete the fact.

6 x 5 ___ __0	6 x ___ ___ 24	6 x 12 ___ 7__	6 x __ ___ 6
6 x 1__ ___ 66	6 x 4 ___ 4	6 x 7 ___ 2	6 x 6 ___ 6
6 x 1__ ___ 72	6 x 2 ___ 2	6 x __ ___ 18	6 x 8 ___ 8
6 x __ ___ 24	6 x 6 ___ 6	6 x 3 ___ 8	6 x 2 ___ 1__

Tip!

Did you know that anytime you are multiplying with at least one even number, the product is always even? It's true. What do you get when you multiply an odd number by another odd number?

_____

Super SUDOKU

Name _____ Date _____

Multiplying by 7

Directions

● Every row, column, and 2-by-2 box ⊞ should contain each of these digits:

1 **2** **3** **4**

● Fill in each blank with the correct number to complete the fact.

7 x 1__ —— 77	7 x __ —— 28	7 x 5 —— __5	7 x 6 —— 4__
7 x __ —— 14	7 x __ —— 21	7 x 6 —— __2	7 x __ —— 7
7 x 12 —— 8__	7 x 2 —— __4	7 x 4 —— __8	7 x __ —— 21
7 x 5 —— __5	7 x 3 —— __1	7 x __1 —— 77	7 x 7 —— __9

Tip!

Try to memorize benchmarks to help you. For example, if you know 7 x 5 is 35 then you only have to add one 7 to figure that 7 x 6 = 42. Add another 7 to find 7 x 7 = _____.

Super Sudoku Math: Multiplication & Division Facts • © 2010 by Eric Charlesworth • Scholastic Teaching Resources

Name _____ Date _____

Multiplying by **7**

Directions

● Every row, column, and 2-by-2 box ⊞ should contain each of these digits:

5   6   7   8

● Fill in each blank with the correct number to complete the fact.

7 x 5 — 3 _	7 x __ — 42	7 x 12 — _ 4	__ x 1 — 7
7 x __ — 49	7 x __ — 56	7 x 9 — _ 3	7 x 8 — _ 6
7 x __ — 56	7 x __ — 35	__ x 11 — 77	7 x __ — 42
7 x 9 — _ 3	7 x 11 — _ 7	7 x 8 — _ 6	7 x 4 — 2 _

Word Problem

Touchdowns are worth 7 points and field goals are worth 3 points. If the Eagles scored 31 points in their last game, how many touchdowns and field goals do you think they scored?

_____

Super Sudoku Math: Multiplication & Division Facts • © 2010 by Eric Charlesworth • Scholastic Teaching Resources

15

Super SUDOKU

Name _____   Date _____

Multiplying by 5, 6, and 7

Directions

● Every row, column, and 3-by-2 box ⊞ should contain each of these digits:

1	2	3	4	5	6

● Fill in each blank with the correct number to complete the fact.

5 x 7 ――― 3 _	5 x __ ――― 30	6 x 4 ――― _ 4	7 x __ ――― 7	7 x 6 ――― _ 2	7 x 5 ――― _ 5
6 x __ ――― 24	7 x __ ――― 21	6 x 3 ――― _ 8	5 x 5 ――― _ 5	5 x 9 ――― 4 _	7 x 9 ――― _ 3
5 x 12 ――― _ 0	5 x 11 ――― _ 5	6 x 8 ――― _ 8	7 x 9 ――― 6 _	6 x 12 ――― 7 _	6 x __ ――― _ 6
5 x __ ――― 10	7 x 3 ――― 2 _	6 x 6 ――― _ 6	6 x __ ――― 30	7 x __ ――― 42	6 x 8 ――― _ 8
5 x __ ――― 15	5 x 8 ――― _ 0	7 x 8 ――― _ 6	7 x 8 ――― 5 _	6 x 2 ――― _ 2	7 x 4 ――― _ 8
7 x 2 ――― _ 4	5 x 4 ――― _ 0	6 x 11 ――― _ 6	7 x 12 ――― 8 _	6 x __ ――― 18	5 x 11 ――― 5 _

Super Sudoku Math: Multiplication & Division Facts • © 2010 by Eric Charlesworth • Scholastic Teaching Resources

Super SUDOKU

Name _____ Date _____

Multiplying by 8

Directions

● Every row, column, and 2-by-2 box ⊞ should contain each of these digits:

1   2   3   4

● Fill in each blank with the correct number to complete the fact.

8 x 1 __ ___ 96	8 x __ ___ 24	8 x 6 ___ _ 8	8 x 1 __ ___ 88
8 x __ ___ 8	8 x 5 ___ _ 0	8 x __ ___ 16	8 x 4 ___ _ 2
8 x __ ___ 24	8 x 9 ___ 7 __	8 x __ 2 ___ 96	8 x 6 ___ _ 8
8 x __ ___ 32	8 x 2 ___ _ 6	8 x 4 ___ _ 2	8 x 3 ___ _ 4

Word Problem

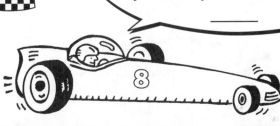

My friend Sally went running for 8 straight days. If she ran for 6 miles each day, how many miles did she run total?

_____

Super Sudoku Math: Multiplication & Division Facts • © 2010 by Eric Charlesworth • Scholastic Teaching Resources

Name _____ Date _____

Multiplying by 8

Directions

● Every row, column, and 2-by-2 box ⊞ should contain each of these digits:

5   6   7   8

● Fill in each blank with the correct number to complete the fact.

8 x __ —— 40	8 x 2 —— 1 __	8 x 11 —— __ 8	8 x __ —— 56
8 x 9 —— __ 2	8 x 10 —— __ 0	8 x __ —— 48	8 x 7 —— __ 6
8 x 6 —— 4 __	8 x 7 —— __ 6	8 x 9 —— __ 2	8 x 12 —— 9 __
8 x 8 —— __ 4	8 x __ —— 56	8 x __ —— 40	8 x __ —— 64

Tip!

Want a smart way to multiply a number by 8?
You can do it by doubling your number three times.
That's because 2 x 2 x 2 = 8. Try that strategy to
find the answer to 25 x 8.

_____

Super Sudoku Math: Multiplication & Division Facts • © 2010 by Eric Charlesworth • Scholastic Teaching Resources

Super SUDOKU

Multiplying by **9**

Directions

● Every row, column, and 2-by-2 box ⊞ should contain each of these digits:

1 **2** **3** **4**

● Fill in each blank with the correct number to complete the fact.

9 x 4 _ 6	9 x 5 _ 5	9 x 3 _ 7	9 x 9 8_
9 x 1_ 99	9 x _ 18	9 x _ 36	9 x 7 6_
9 x 1_ 108	9 x _ 9	9 x _ 27	9 x 6 5_
9 x 5 _ 5	9 x 7 6_	9 x _2 108	9 x 8 7_

Tip!

There are lots of tricks for multiplying by 9. One strategy is to first multiply the number by 10 (just add a zero!) and then subtract the number from your answer.

Super Sudoku Math: Multiplication & Division Facts • © 2010 by Eric Charlesworth • Scholastic Teaching Resources

Super SUDOKU

Name _____ Date _____

Multiplying by 9

Directions

● Every row, column, and 2-by-2 box ⊞ should contain each of these digits:

| 5 | 6 | 7 | 8 |

● Fill in each blank with the correct number to complete the fact.

9 x 6 ___ 4	9 x 7 ___ 3	9 x ___ 63	9 x 12 10 ___
9 x ___ 63	9 x 9 ___ 1	9 x ___ 54	9 x 5 4 ___
9 x ___ 72	9 x 3 2 ___	9 x 6 ___ 4	9 x 7 ___ 3
9 x ___ 54	9 x ___ 45	9 x 9 ___ 1	9 x 8 ___ 2

Tip!

When you multiply 9 by another one-digit number, the sum of the two digits in your answer will always add up to 9. Try it: 9 x 3 = 27. Now add the digits in the answer: 2 + 7 = 9. Cool!

Super Sudoku Math: Multiplication & Division Facts • © 2010 by Eric Charlesworth • Scholastic Teaching Resources

Name _____   Date _____

Multiplying by 8 and 9

Directions

- Every row, column, and 3-by-2 box ⊞ should contain each of these digits:

  1   2   3   4   5   6

- Fill in each blank with the correct number to complete the fact.

9 x __ 54	8 x __ 24	9 x __ 45	8 x __ 8	8 x 3 _4	8 x 5 _0
8 x __ 16	9 x 9 8_	9 x __ 36	8 x __ 48	9 x __ 27	9 x 6 _4
9 x 7 6_	8 x 6 _8	9 x 7 _3	8 x 7 _6	9 x 2 _8	8 x __ 16
9 x 2 _8	8 x 7 _6	9 x 3 _7	8 x __ 24	9 x 5 _5	8 x 2 1_
8 x 6 _8	8 x 8 _4	8 x 4 _2	9 x 3 _7	8 x __ 40	9 x 9 8_
9 x 6 _4	8 x 4 3_	9 x 12 _08	9 x 5 _5	9 x 4 3_	9 x 4 _6

Super Sudoku Math: Multiplication & Division Facts • © 2010 by Eric Charlesworth • Scholastic Teaching Resources

Name _____ Date _____

Multiplying by **10**

Directions

● Every row, column, and 2-by-2 box ⊞ should contain each of these digits:

1 **2** **3** **4**

● Fill in each blank with the correct number to complete the fact.

10 x ___ — 10	10 x 4 — ___0	10 x ___ — 30	10 x 12 — 1_0
10 x 2 — ___0	10 x 3 — ___0	10 x ___ — 40	10 x 12 — _20
10 x ___ — 40	10 x 1 — ___0	10 x ___ — 20	10 x ___ — 30
10 x 3 — ___0	10 x 1_ — 120	10 x 10 — _00	10 x 4 — ___0

Tip!

Here's a rhyme for you. When multiplying a whole number by 10, you can always be a hero. It's very simple. Just add a zero!

Super Sudoku Math: Multiplication & Division Facts • © 2010 by Eric Charlesworth • Scholastic Teaching Resources

Name _____ Date _____

Multiplying by 11

Directions

- Every row, column, and 2-by-2 box ⊞ should contain each of these digits:

  1 **2** **3** **4**

- Fill in each blank with the correct number to complete the fact.

11 x __ 22	11 x 3 3_	11 x __ 44	_1 x 7 77
1_ x 6 66	11 x 4 _4	11 x 2 _2	11 x __ 33
11 x __ 33	11 x 12 13_	11 x 1 1_	11 x 4 4_
11 x __ 44	11 x 11 12_	11 x 3 3_	11 x 1_ 132

Tip!

Here's a super-easy way to multiply by 11:
First, multiply by 10. Then add one more of
your number. For example, To find 5 x 11, think
5 x 10 = 50 and 50 + 5 = 55. What's 40 x 11?

_____

Super SUDOKU

Name _____ Date _____

Multiplying by **12**

Directions

● Every row, column, and 2-by-2 box ⊞ should contain each of these digits:

1   2   3   4

● Fill in each blank with the correct number to complete the fact.

12 x 4 _ 8	12 x 3 _ 6	12 x 6 7 _	12 x 1 _ 2
12 x 9 _08	12 x 11 13_	12 x __ 48	12 x __ 36
12 x __ 36	12 x 7 8_	12 x 10 _20	12 x 2 _ 4
12 x __ 24	_2 x 8 96	12 x 3 _ 6	12 x 12 14_

Word Problem

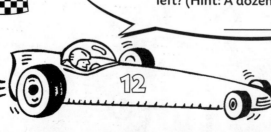

Missy bought 7 dozen eggs but 5 eggs broke on the way home. How many eggs did she have left? (Hint: A dozen means 12.)

_____

24

Super Sudoku Math: Multiplication & Division Facts • © 2010 by Eric Charlesworth • Scholastic Teaching Resources

Super SUDOKU

Name _____ Date _____

Multiplying by 10, 11, and 12

Directions

● Every row, column, and 3-by-2 box ⊞ should contain each of these digits:

1 2 3 4 5 6

● Fill in each blank with the correct number to complete the fact.

10 x 3 _0	11 x __ 66	12 x __ 24	12 x __ 48	10 x __ 10	10 x __ 50
12 x 12 _44	11 x 4 4_	11 x __ 55	12 x 11 13_	12 x 5 _0	12 x 3 _6
11 x __ 22	10 x 5 _0	11 x 12 _32	10 x __ 60	10 x __ 30	11 x __ 44
12 x 4 _8	11 x __ 33	11 x __ 66	10 x __ 50	11 x __ 22	11 x 10 1_0
12 x __ 72	11 x 1_ 121	12 x 12 1_4	10 x __ 30	12 x __ 60	12 x 10 1_0
11 x __ 55	10 x __ 20	12 x 3 _6	12 x __ 12	12 x 7 8_	12 x 8 9_

Name _____ Date _____

Dividing by **1**

Directions

● Every row, column, and 2-by-2 box ⊞ should contain each of these digits:

1	**2**	**3**	**4**

● Fill in each blank with the correct number to complete the fact.

$8 \div \underline{\ \ } = 8$	$\underline{\ \ } \div 1 = 4$	$\underline{\ \ } \div 1 = 3$	$2 \div 1 = \underline{\ \ }$
$1\underline{\ \ } \div 1 = 12$	$3 \div 1 = \underline{\ \ }$	$4 \div 1 = \underline{\ \ }$	$9 \div \underline{\ \ } = 9$
$4 \div 1 = \underline{\ \ }$	$6 \div \underline{\ \ } = 6$	$1\underline{\ \ } \div 1 = 12$	$3 \div 1 = \underline{\ \ }$
$\underline{\ \ } \div 1 = 3$	$\underline{\ \ } \div 1 = 2$	$10 \div \underline{\ \ } = 10$	$\underline{\ \ } \div 1 = 4$

Word Problem

Just like multiplying by one, dividing by one will give you the number you started with. What's 17 bazookazillion divided by one?

_____

Super Sudoku Math: Multiplication & Division Facts • © 2010 by Eric Charlesworth • Scholastic Teaching Resources

Name _____ Date _____

Dividing by **2**

Directions

- Every row, column, and 2-by-2 box ⊞ should contain each of these digits:

    1   **2**   **3**   **4**

- Fill in each blank with the correct number to complete the fact.

__6 ÷ 2 = 8	1__ ÷ 2 = 7	6 ÷ 2 = __	__0 ÷ 2 = 10
__4 ÷ 2 = 12	6 ÷ 2 = __	2__ ÷ 2 = 12	__0 ÷ 2 = 5
__ ÷ 2 = 2	__4 ÷ 2 = 7	__2 ÷ 2 = 11	6 ÷ 2 = __
6 ÷ 2 = __	1__ ÷ 2 = 6	__2 ÷ 2 = 6	8 ÷ 2 = __

Tip!

Dividing by 2 is the same as splitting a number in half, so it is called halving a number. What do you get when you halve 100?

_____

Name _____ Date _____

Dividing by **3**

Directions

● Every row, column, and 2-by-2 box ⊞ should contain each of these digits:

1　**2**　**3**　**4**

● Fill in each blank with the correct number to complete the fact.

9 ÷ 3 = __	__8 ÷ 3 = 6	2__ ÷ 3 = 8	6 ÷ __ = 3
__4 ÷ 3 = 8	12 ÷ 3 = __	3 ÷ 3 = __	__0 ÷ 10 = 3
12 ÷ 3 = __	__7 ÷ 3 = 9	__3 ÷ 3 = 11	__2 ÷ 3 = 4
__5 ÷ 3 = 5	__6 ÷ 3 = 12	__1 ÷ 3 = 7	2__ ÷ 3 = 8

Word Problem

Three students are making posters. They decide to share a box of 24 markers equally. How many markers does each student get to use?

_____

Name _____ Date _____

Dividing by **4**

Directions

● Every row, column, and 2-by-2 box ⊞ should contain each of these digits:

1 **2** **3** **4**

● Fill in each blank with the correct number to complete the fact.

4 ÷ ___ = 1	___2 ÷ 4 = 8	___8 ÷ 4 = 7	48 ÷ 4 = ___2
___6 ÷ 4 = 4	___8 ÷ 4 = 7	8 ÷ ___ = 2	___6 ÷ 4 = 9
___6 ÷ 4 = 9	2___ ÷ 4 = 6	4 ÷ 4 = ___	3___ ÷ 4 = 8
___0 ÷ 4 = 5	44 ÷ 4 = 1___	12 ÷ 4 = ___	16 ÷ 4 = ___

Tip!

To divide by 4 you simply split a number in half and then do it again. Can you use that strategy to divide 800 by 4?

800 ÷ 4 = _____

Super SUDOKU

Name _____ Date _____

Dividing by **1, 2, 3,** and **4**

Directions

- Every row, column, and 3-by-2 box ⊞ should contain each of these digits:

  1 **2** **3** **4** **5** **6**

- Fill in each blank with the correct number to complete the fact.

$4\overline{)3\_}$ ⁹	$\_\overline{)3}$ ¹	$1\overline{)5}$	$4\overline{)4}$	$\_\overline{)20}$ ¹⁰	$4\overline{)2\_}$ ⁶
$4\overline{)3\_}$ ⁸	$3\overline{)\_8}$ ⁶	$4\overline{)4\_}$ ¹¹	$2\overline{)1\_}$ ⁸	$3\overline{)3\_}$ ¹¹	$4\overline{)20}$
$4\overline{)12}$	$\_\overline{)48}$ ¹²	$1\overline{)6}$	$3\overline{)1\_}$ ⁵	$2\overline{)24}$ ²	$\_\overline{)6}$ ³
$\_\overline{)11}$ ¹¹	$2\overline{)10}$	$3\overline{)36}$ ¹⁻	$\_\overline{)21}$ ⁷	$\_\overline{)40}$ ¹⁰	$2\overline{)12}$
$\_\overline{)32}$ ⁸	$4\overline{)1\_}$ ⁴	$\_\overline{)9}$ ³	$10\overline{)20}$	$3\overline{)15}$	$3\overline{)30}$ ⁻⁰
$4\overline{)20}$	$\_\overline{)14}$ ⁷	$\_\overline{)8}$ ⁸	$\_\overline{)28}$ ⁷	$3\overline{)18}$	$4\overline{)\_6}$ ⁹

Super Sudoku Math: Multiplication & Division Facts • © 2010 by Eric Charlesworth • Scholastic Teaching Resources

Super SUDOKU

Name _____ Date _____

Dividing by 5

Directions

● Every row, column, and 2-by-2 box ⊞ should contain each of these digits:

1   2   3   4

● Fill in each blank with the correct number to complete the fact.

__5 ÷ 5 = 5	__5 ÷ 5 = 7	__0 ÷ 5 = 8	__0 ÷ 5 = 2
5 ÷ 5 = __	20 ÷ 5 = __	10 ÷ 5 = __	__0 ÷ 5 = 6
15 ÷ 5 = __	__0 ÷ 5 = 4	__5 ÷ 5 = 3	__5 ÷ 5 = 9
__0 ÷ 5 = 8	55 ÷ 5 = 1__	__5 ÷ 5 = 7	60 ÷ 5 = 1__

Tip!

A number will only divide by 5 evenly if that number ends in 5 or 0. What happens if you try to divide 27 by 5?

_____

Super SUDOKU

Name _____ Date _____

Dividing by 6

Directions

- Every row, column, and 2-by-2 box ⊞ should contain each of these digits:

  1 **2** **3** **4**

- Fill in each blank with the correct number to complete the fact.

__2 ÷ 6 = 7	18 ÷ 6 = __	12 ÷ 6 = __	72 ÷ 6 = __2
__2 ÷ 6 = 2	__4 ÷ 6 = 4	5__ ÷ 6 = 9	__6 ÷ 6 = 6
__0 ÷ 6 = 5	__8 ÷ 6 = 8	66 ÷ 6 = 1__	72 ÷ 6 = 1__
12 ÷ 6 = __	__8 ÷ 6 = 3	18 ÷ 6 = __	24 ÷ 6 = __

Word Problem

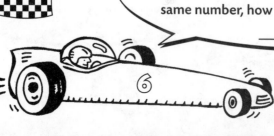

Mya has 18 chocolate kisses and wants to give them to six friends. If she gives each friend the same number, how many does each one get?

_____

Super Sudoku Math: Multiplication & Division Facts • © 2010 by Eric Charlesworth • Scholastic Teaching Resources

Name _____ Date _____

Dividing by **7**

Directions

● Every row, column, and 2-by-2 box ⊞ should contain each of these digits:

5   **6**   **7**   **8**

● Fill in each blank with the correct number to complete the fact.

__6 ÷ 7 = 8	42 ÷ 7 = __	__4 ÷ 7 = 12	__0 ÷ 7 = 10
21 ÷ __ = 3	56 ÷ 7 = __	__3 ÷ 7 = 9	35 ÷ 7 = __
2__ ÷ 7 = 4	3__ ÷ 7 = 5	7__ ÷ 11 = 7	42 ÷ 7 = __
__3 ÷ 7 = 9	14 ÷ __ = 2	__6 ÷ 7 = 8	56 ÷ 7 = __

Tip!

Here's a cheer for you: *5, 6, 7, 8!*
56 divided by 7 is 8!
Isn't that great?

Super SUDOKU

Name _____ Date _____

Dividing by **8**

Directions

● Every row, column, and 2-by-2 box ⊞ should contain each of these digits:

5 6 7 8

● Fill in each blank with the correct number to complete the fact.

40 ÷ 8 = __	__4 ÷ 8 = 8	56 ÷ 8 = __	32 ÷ __ = 4
__2 ÷ 8 = 9	8__ ÷ 11 = 8	48 ÷ 8 = __	40 ÷ 8 = __
__0 ÷ 8 = 10	__2 ÷ 8 = 9	__6 ÷ 8 = 7	9__ ÷ 8 = 12
1__ ÷ 2 = 8	__6 ÷ 8 = 7	24 ÷ __ = 3	56 ÷ 8 = __

Tip!

If multiplying by 8 is really doubling three times, what can you do to divide by 8?

_____

Super Sudoku Math: Multiplication & Division Facts • © 2010 by Eric Charlesworth • Scholastic Teaching Resources

Super SUDOKU

Name _____ Date _____

Dividing by **5, 6, 7,** and **8**

Directions

● Every row, column, and 3-by-2 box ⊞ should contain each of these digits:

1   2   3   4   5   6

● Fill in each blank with the correct number to complete the fact.

5 __)30	9 __)45	2 5)60	5)10	8)24	2 7)1_
7)28	6)12	4 8)_2	3 6)_8	6)36	5)25
7)21	8 8)_4	8 __)40	6)24	12 6)7_	8)8
8)16	1_ 8)88	11 __)44	7)42	7 __)35	5)15
11 __)55	8 6)_8	9 __)54	8)24	7)7	4 6)_4
2 7)84	9 7)6_	6)12	7 8)_6	6 8)_8	7 __)42

Super Sudoku Math: Multiplication & Division Facts • © 2010 by Eric Charlesworth • Scholastic Teaching Resources

35

Super SUDOKU

Name _____ Date _____

Dividing by 9

Directions

- Every row, column, and 2-by-2 box ⊞ should contain each of these digits:

  1 **2** **3** **4**

- Fill in each blank with the correct number to complete the fact.

$9\overline{)7\_}$ ⁸	$9\overline{)\_6}$ ⁴	$9\overline{)\_5}$ ⁵	$9\overline{)8\_}$ ⁹
$9\overline{)\_8}$ ²	$9\overline{)36}$	$9\overline{)18}$	$9\overline{)27}$
$9\overline{)27}$	$9\overline{)7\_}$ ⁸	$9\overline{)90}$ ⁰	$9\overline{)5\_}$ ⁶
$9\overline{)5\_}$ ⁶	$9\overline{)8\_}$ ⁹	$9\overline{)\_6}$ ⁴	$9\overline{)108}$ ¹_

Word Problem

Last week it took Junior 27 minutes to drive 9 laps and he was going the same speed the whole time. How many minutes did each lap take?

_____

Super Sudoku Math: Multiplication & Division Facts • © 2010 by Eric Charlesworth • Scholastic Teaching Resources

Name _____ Date _____

Dividing by **10**

Directions

● Every row, column, and 2-by-2 box ⊞ should contain each of these digits:

1   **2**   **3**   **4**

● Fill in each blank with the correct number to complete the fact.

$10\overline{)40}$	$10\overline{)\_\,0}^{\;3}$	$10\overline{)20}$	$10\overline{)10}^{\;\_\,0}$
$10\overline{)1\_\,0}^{\;11}$	$2\overline{)\_\,0}^{\;2}$	$10\overline{)40}$	$10\overline{)30}$
$10\overline{)30}$	$10\overline{)\_\,0}^{\;4}$	$10\overline{)100}^{\;\_\,0}$	$10\overline{)120}^{\;1_} $
$10\overline{)1\_\,0}^{\;12}$	$\_\,0\overline{)60}^{\;6}$	$10\overline{)\_\,0}^{\;3}$	$10\overline{)\_\,0}^{\;4}$

Tip!

If a number can be divided by 10 evenly then it must
end in zero. To divide by 10, simply take off the last zero.
What do you get when you divide 240 by 10?

_____

Super SUDOKU

Name _____ Date _____

Dividing by **11**

Directions

● Every row, column, and 2-by-2 box ⊞ should contain each of these digits:

1 **2** **3** **4**

● Fill in each blank with the correct number to complete the fact.

$11\overline{)33}$	$11\overline{)\underline{}4}^{\,4}$	$11\overline{)22}$	$11\overline{)1\underline{}0}^{\,10}$
$11\overline{)132}^{\,\underline{}2}$	$11\overline{)\underline{}2}^{\,2}$	$11\overline{)4\underline{}}^{\,4}$	$11\overline{)3\underline{}}^{\,3}$
$11\overline{)1\underline{}1}^{\,11}$	$11\overline{)11}$	$11\overline{)33}$	$11\overline{)44}$
$11\overline{)44}$	$11\overline{)\underline{}3}^{\,3}$	$11\overline{)110}^{\,\underline{}0}$	$11\overline{)22}$

Word Problem

Over a period of 11 months, Jorge read 44 books. How many books did he read per month?

_____

Super Sudoku Math: Multiplication & Division Facts • © 2010 by Eric Charlesworth • Scholastic Teaching Resources

Name _____ Date _____

Dividing by **12**

Directions

● Every row, column, and 2-by-2 box ⊞ should contain each of these digits:

1　**2**　**3**　**4**

● Fill in each blank with the correct number to complete the fact.

12$\overline{)12}$	12$\overline{)48}$	$\overset{3}{12\overline{)\_6}}$	$\overset{8}{1\_\overline{)96}}$
$\overset{5}{1\_\overline{)60}}$	12$\overline{)36}$	12$\overline{)48}$	$\overset{12}{12\overline{)\_44}}$
$\overset{12}{12\overline{)1\_4}}$	12$\overline{)12}$	12$\overline{)24}$	$\overset{3}{12\overline{)\_6}}$
$\overset{11}{12\overline{)1\_2}}$	$\overset{6}{12\overline{)7\_}}$	$\overset{0}{12\overline{)120}}$	$\overset{7}{12\overline{)8\_}}$

Word Problem

A group of 72 people traveled to an amusement park in 12 shuttle buses. If each shuttle bus had the same number of people, how many people were in each vehicle?

_____

Super SUDOKU

Name _____ Date _____

Dividing by 9, 10, 11, and 12

Directions

- Every row, column, and 3-by-2 box ⊞ should contain each of these digits:

1 2 3 4 5 6

- Fill in each blank with the correct number to complete the fact.

$9\overline{)18}$	$12\overline{)48}$	$12\overline{)36}$	$10\overline{)10}$	$9\overline{)45}$	$11\overline{)66}$
$9\overline{)\_4}^{\,6}$	$9\overline{)\_8}^{\,2}$	$12\overline{)3\_}^{\,3}$	$11\overline{)33}$	$10\overline{)20}$	$12\overline{)1\_4}^{\,12}$
$9\overline{)\_6}^{\,4}$	$9\overline{)\_7}^{\,3}$	$9\overline{)8\_}^{\,9}$	$11\overline{)44}$	$12\overline{)\_0}^{\,5}$	$9\overline{)\_4}^{\,6}$
$10\overline{)40}$	$\_\overline{)72}^{\,12}$	$11\overline{)55}$	$11\overline{)22}$	$9\overline{)27}$	$\_0\overline{)10}^{\,1}$
$12\overline{)9\_}^{\,8}$	$10\overline{)30}$	$11\overline{)44}$	$12\overline{)60}$	$9\overline{)99}^{\,1\_}$	$1\_\overline{)48}^{\,4}$
$\_1\overline{)132}^{\,12}$	$9\overline{)45}$	$1\_\overline{)24}^{\,2}$	$10\overline{)60}$	$7\overline{)8\_}^{\,12}$	$9\overline{)\_6}^{\,4}$

Super Sudoku Math: Multiplication & Division Facts • © 2010 by Eric Charlesworth • Scholastic Teaching Resources

Super SUDOKU

Name _____ Date _____

Multiplying by 1–12

Directions

● Every row, column, and 3-by-2 box ⊞ should contain each of these digits:

1 2 3 4 5 6

● Fill in each blank with the correct number to complete the fact.

5 x 8 _0	8 x 12 9_	7 x __ 14	6 x 3 _8	9 x 4 _6	11 x __ 55
9 x 9 8_	3 x __ 15	3 x 11 3_	7 x __ 28	9 x __ 18	4 x 4 1_
10 x __ 60	10 x __ 30	9 x __ 45	8 x 3 _4	11 x 1 _1	12 x __ 48
5 x 4 _0	12 x 12 _44	8 x __ 32	9 x __ 54	8 x 7 _6	6 x 5 _0
12 x __ 60	3 x __ 6	8 x __ 48	9 x 7 6_	11 x 4 4_	8 x 2 _6
9 x __ 27	9 x 5 _5	8 x _0 80	2 x __ 10	8 x 8 _4	5 x 5 _5

Super Sudoku Math: Multiplication & Division Facts • © 2010 by Eric Charlesworth • Scholastic Teaching Resources

41

Name _____ Date _____

Multiplying by **1–12**

Directions

- Every row, column, and 3-by-2 box ⊞ should contain each of these digits:

1 **2** **3** **4** **5** **6**

- Fill in each blank with the correct number to complete the fact.

8 x __ ___ 40	9 x __ ___ 54	3 x __ ___ 6	7 x __ ___ 7	11 x __ ___ 44	12 x __ ___ 36
7 x 2 ___ 1_	9 x 4 ___ _6	9 x 2 ___ _8	8 x 3 ___ _4	9 x 6 ___ _4	8 x __ ___ 48
11 x 6 ___ 6_	4 x __ ___ 20	7 x 7 ___ _9	12 x 11 ___ 1_2	6 x __ ___ 12	7 x 3 ___ 2_
8 x __ ___ 16	9 x 12 ___ _08	5 x 7 ___ _5	6 x __ ___ 30	8 x __ ___ 48	10 x 4 ___ _0
9 x 7 ___ 6_	11 x 4 ___ 4_	5 x __ ___ 25	6 x __ ___ 36	1 x __ ___ 1	11 x __ ___ 22
12 x 10 ___ _20	12 x 6 ___ 7_	8 x 7 ___ 5_	7 x 6 ___ _2	11 x __ ___ 33	10 x __ ___ 50

Super Sudoku Math: Multiplication & Division Facts • © 2010 by Eric Charlesworth • Scholastic Teaching Resources

Name _____ Date _____

Dividing by **1–12**

Directions

- Every row, column, and 3-by-2 box ⊞ should contain each of these digits:

1 2 3 4 5 6

- Fill in each blank with the correct number to complete the fact.

$7\overline{)7}$	$7\overline{)42}$	$\underline{}\overline{)10}$ → 2	$\underline{}\overline{)4}$ → 1	$\underline{}\overline{)12}$ → 6	$4\overline{)\underline{}6}$ → 9
$\underline{}\overline{)24}$ → 12	$\underline{}\overline{)40}$ → 10	$9\overline{)27}$	$9\overline{)54}$	$11\overline{)\underline{}5}$ → 5	$7\overline{)2\underline{}}$ → 3
$\underline{}\overline{)24}$ → 8	$\underline{}\overline{)20}$ → 4	$4\overline{)3\underline{}}$ → 8	$9\overline{)8\underline{}}$ → 9	$7\overline{)8\underline{}}$ → 12	$8\overline{)5\underline{}}$ → 7
$8\overline{)48}$	$12\overline{)12}$	$9\overline{)\underline{}5}$ → 5	$\underline{}\overline{)30}$ → 6	$\underline{}\overline{)18}$ → 6	$\underline{}\overline{)14}$ → 7
$\underline{}\overline{)55}$ → 11	$8\overline{)\underline{}4}$ → 3	$12\overline{)9\underline{}}$ → 8	$\underline{}\overline{)9}$ → 3	$\underline{}\overline{)8}$ → 8	$\underline{}\overline{)40}$ → 10
$3\overline{)12}$	$9\overline{)6\underline{}}$ → 7	$3\overline{)33}$ → 1_	$8\overline{)16}$	$1\overline{)\underline{}}$ → 6	$\underline{}\overline{)40}$ → 8

Super SUDOKU

Name _____ Date _____

Dividing by 1–12

Directions

● Every row, column, and 3-by-2 box ⊞ should contain each of these digits:

| 1 | 2 | 3 | 4 | 5 | 6 |

● Fill in each blank with the correct number to complete the fact.

$6\overline{)36}$	$6\overline{)30}$	$9\overline{)9}$	$6\overline{)7\_}^{\,12}$	$4\overline{)12}$	$\_\overline{)16}^{\,4}$
$\_\overline{)48}^{\,12}$	$\_\overline{)20}^{\,10}$	$\_\overline{)18}^{\,6}$	$9\overline{)99}^{\,1\_}$	$\_\overline{)54}^{\,9}$	$7\overline{)35}$
$9\overline{)27}$	$6\overline{)6\_}^{\,11}$	$\_\overline{)40}^{\,8}$	$7\overline{)\_9}^{\,7}$	$\_\overline{)22}^{\,11}$	$7\overline{)70}^{\,\_0}$
$8\overline{)16}$	$11\overline{)11}$	$12\overline{)14\_}^{\,12}$	$\_\overline{)42}^{\,7}$	$8\overline{)\_6}^{\,7}$	$7\overline{)21}$
$9\overline{)45}$	$2\overline{)8}$	$\_\overline{)24}^{\,4}$	$7\overline{)6\_}^{\,9}$	$\_\overline{)8}^{\,8}$	$8\overline{)3\_}^{\,4}$
$9\overline{)\_08}^{\,12}$	$4\overline{)\_2}^{\,8}$	$\_\overline{)18}^{\,9}$	$\_\overline{)50}^{\,10}$	$7\overline{)28}$	$\_\overline{)54}^{\,9}$

Super Sudoku Math: Multiplication & Division Facts • © 2010 by Eric Charlesworth • Scholastic Teaching Resources

Name _____ Date _____

Full Review

Directions

● Every row, column, and 3-by-2 box ⊞ should contain each of these digits:

1 2 3 4 5 6

● Fill in each blank with the correct number to complete the fact.

$\dfrac{10}{\underline{}\,\overline{)20}}$	$\dfrac{\underline{}2}{12\,\overline{)144}}$	$9\,\overline{)36}$	$\begin{array}{r}5\\ \times\ \underline{}\\ \hline 30\end{array}$	$\begin{array}{r}11\\ \times\ \underline{}\\ \hline 33\end{array}$	$\begin{array}{r}6\\ \times\ 9\\ \hline \underline{}4\end{array}$
$\dfrac{7}{8\,\overline{)5\underline{}}}$	$\dfrac{6}{\underline{}\,\overline{)18}}$	$8\,\overline{)40}$	$\begin{array}{r}8\\ \times\ 3\\ \hline 2\underline{}\end{array}$	$\begin{array}{r}12\\ \times\ \underline{}\\ \hline 12\end{array}$	$\begin{array}{r}7\\ \times\ \underline{}\\ \hline 14\end{array}$
$\begin{array}{r}12\\ \times\ 9\\ \hline \underline{}08\end{array}$	$\begin{array}{r}6\\ \times\ \underline{}\\ \hline 36\end{array}$	$\begin{array}{r}9\\ \times\ \underline{}\\ \hline 18\end{array}$	$\dfrac{5}{\underline{}\,\overline{)25}}$	$10\,\overline{)40}$	$9\,\overline{)27}$
$\begin{array}{r}9\\ \times\ 5\\ \hline \underline{}5\end{array}$	$\begin{array}{r}9\\ \times\ 6\\ \hline \underline{}4\end{array}$	$\begin{array}{r}9\\ \times\ 7\\ \hline 6\underline{}\end{array}$	$12\,\overline{)24}$	$\dfrac{4}{\underline{}\,\overline{)24}}$	$\dfrac{1}{\underline{}\,\overline{)1}}$
$4\,\overline{)12}$	$\dfrac{3}{7\,\overline{)\underline{}1}}$	$\dfrac{8}{2\,\overline{)1\underline{}}}$	$\begin{array}{r}6\\ \times\ \underline{}2\\ \hline 72\end{array}$	$\begin{array}{r}3\\ \times\ \underline{}\\ \hline 15\end{array}$	$\begin{array}{r}8\\ \times\ \underline{}\\ \hline 32\end{array}$
$\dfrac{5}{11\,\overline{)5\underline{}}}$	$7\,\overline{)28}$	$\dfrac{\underline{}0}{7\,\overline{)70}}$	$\begin{array}{r}5\\ \times\ \underline{}\\ \hline 15\end{array}$	$\begin{array}{r}10\\ \times\ \underline{}\\ \hline 20\end{array}$	$\begin{array}{r}8\\ \times\ 8\\ \hline \underline{}4\end{array}$

Super SUDOKU

Name _____ Date _____

Full Review

Directions

● Every row, column, and 3-by-2 box ⊞ should contain each of these digits:

1 2 3 4 5 6

● Fill in each blank with the correct number to complete the fact.

$8 \times \underline{} = 24$	$6 \times \underline{} = 36$	$9 \times 3 = \underline{}7$	$11 \times 4 = \underline{}4$	$5 \times 2 = \underline{}0$	$5 \times 5 = 2\underline{}$
$6\overline{)60} = \underline{}0$	$\underline{}\overline{)20} = 5$	$\underline{}\overline{)20} = 4$	$8\overline{)3\underline{}} = 4$	$\underline{}\overline{)72} = 12$	$\underline{}\overline{)15} = 5$
$8 \times 9 = 7\underline{}$	$6 \times 9 = \underline{}4$	$9 \times 9 = 8\underline{}$	$8 \times 7 = 5\underline{}$	$12 \times 3 = \underline{}6$	$4 \times \underline{} = 16$
$6\overline{)\underline{}8} = 8$	$\underline{}\overline{)9} = 3$	$\underline{}\overline{)12} = 2$	$5\overline{)\underline{}} = 1$	$7\overline{)4\underline{}} = 6$	$9\overline{)8\underline{}} = 9$
$9 \times 7 = \underline{}3$	$2 \times \underline{} = 2$	$3 \times \underline{} = 12$	$9 \times 4 = \underline{}6$	$7 \times \underline{} = 35$	$10 \times \underline{} = 20$
$11\overline{)55}$	$4\overline{)8}$	$11\overline{)33}$	$12\overline{)144} = \underline{}2$	$6\overline{)5\underline{}} = 9$	$8\overline{)\underline{}4} = 8$

Super Sudoku Math: Multiplication & Division Facts • © 2010 by Eric Charlesworth • Scholastic Teaching Resources

Full Review

Directions

● Every row, column, and 3-by-2 box ▦ should contain each of these digits:

1	2	3	4	5	6

● Fill in each blank with the correct number to complete the fact.

9 x 6 ——— _ 4	8 x 3 ——— _ 4	8 x 4 ——— _ 2	7 x 6 ——— _ 2	4 x 3 ——— _ 2	9 x 7 ——— _ 3
8 x 2 ——— 1 _	7 x 3 ——— 2 _	7 x 2 ——— 1 _	9 x 7 ——— 6 _	9 x 5 ——— 4 _	9 x 8 ——— 7 _
6 x 5 ——— _ 0	8 x 7 ——— _ 6	1 x 2 ——— _	11 x 11 ——— 12 _	8 x 8 ——— _ 4	8 x 5 ——— _ 0
3⟌12	3⟌18	_ 0 8⟌80	1 _ 12⟌144	9⟌27	8⟌40
8⟌16	10⟌30	8⟌48	5⟌25	8⟌32	7 _⟌7
12⟌12	12 _⟌48	7 _⟌35	2⟌12	6⟌12	11 _⟌33

Answer Key

Page 7

3	1	4	2
2	4	1	3
4	2	3	1
1	3	2	4

Page 8

5	6	8	7
7	8	6	5
8	5	7	6
6	7	5	8

Tip: 12 dollars

Page 9

3	1	4	2
2	4	1	3
4	2	3	1
1	3	2	4

Tip: 27

Page 10

3	4	2	1
1	2	4	3
2	1	3	4
4	3	1	2

Word Problem: 80

Page 11

2	4	3	1	5	6
5	1	6	3	2	4
3	2	1	4	6	5
4	6	5	2	3	1
6	3	4	5	1	2
1	5	2	6	4	3

Page 12

1	4	3	2
2	3	4	1
4	1	2	3
3	2	1	4

Page 13

3	4	2	1
1	2	4	3
2	1	3	4
4	3	1	2

Tip: You get an odd number.

Page 14

1	4	3	2
2	3	4	1
4	1	2	3
3	2	1	4

Word Problem: 49

Page 15

5	6	8	7
7	8	6	5
8	5	7	6
6	7	5	8

Word Problem: 4 touchdowns and 1 field goal

Page 16

5	6	2	1	4	3
4	3	1	2	5	6
6	5	4	3	2	1
2	1	3	5	6	4
3	4	5	6	1	2
1	2	6	4	3	5

Page 17

2	3	4	1
1	4	2	3
3	2	1	4
4	1	3	2

Word Problem: 48 miles

Page 18

5	6	8	7
7	8	6	5
8	5	7	6
6	7	5	8

Tip: 200

Page 19

3	4	2	1
1	2	4	3
2	1	3	4
4	3	1	2

Page 20

5	6	7	8
7	8	6	5
8	7	5	6
6	5	8	7

Page 21

6	3	5	1	2	4
2	1	4	6	3	5
3	4	6	5	1	2
1	5	2	3	4	6
4	6	3	2	5	1
5	2	1	4	6	3

Page 22

1	4	3	2
2	3	4	1
4	1	2	3
3	2	1	4

Page 23

2	3	4	1
1	4	2	3
3	2	1	4
4	1	3	2

Tip: 440

Page 24

4	3	2	1
1	2	4	3
3	4	1	2
2	1	3	4

Word Problem: 79 eggs

Page 25

3	6	2	4	1	5
1	4	5	2	6	3
2	5	1	6	3	4
4	3	6	5	2	1
6	1	4	3	5	2
5	2	3	1	4	6

Page 26

1	4	3	2
2	3	4	1
4	1	2	3
3	2	1	4

Word Problem: 17 bazookazillion